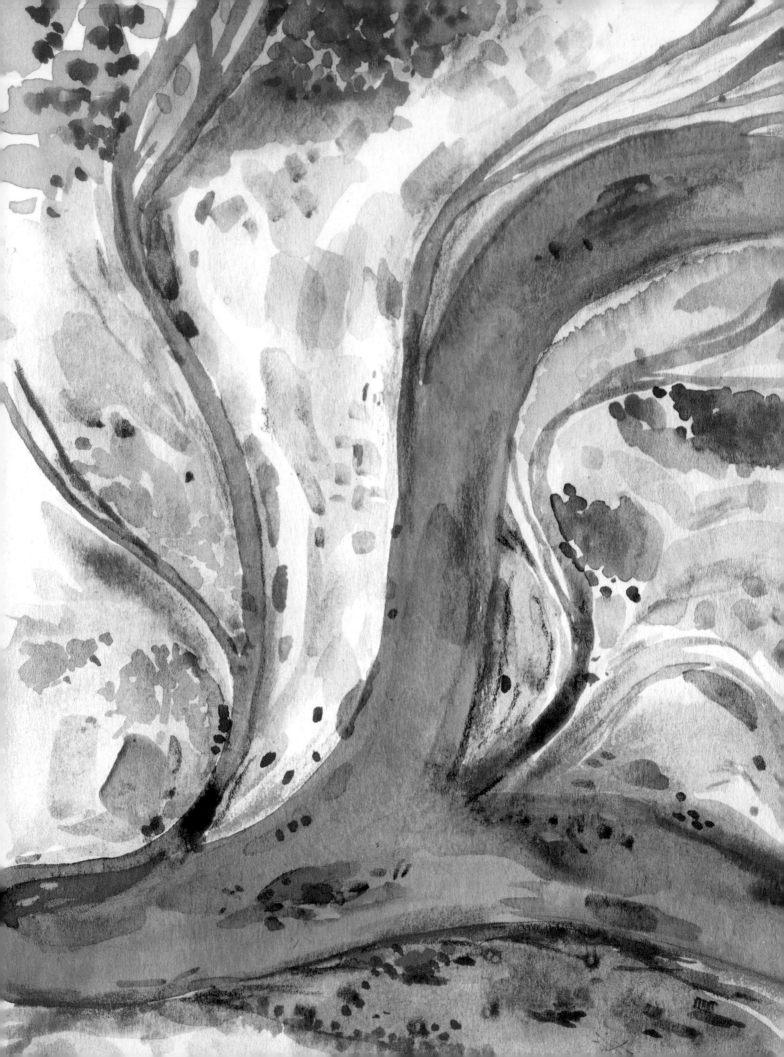

In the northeast of India flows a river so mighty that people who live on its many islands call it a moving ocean. During the monsoon season, the glaciers and the rains feed it more water than it can hold, and the river goes wild. It chews off big chunks of its own islands, strips all vegetation from the remaining land, and sweeps away the soil, destroying property and sometimes lives of people and animals. And when the waters recede, the river renews the earth with its rich silt deposits. The river is both a curse and a blessing.

Rina Singh is an award-winning children's book author and spoken word coach. She has an MFA in creative writing and has written many critically acclaimed books for children. As a writer, she is drawn to real life stories about social justice and the environment. Her books have been translated into multiple languages and have received many starred reviews. Her book "Grandmother School" won the Christie Harris Children's Literature Prize, and "111 Trees" was featured in "The New York Times". A lover of poetry, photography, beautiful books, trees, and monks, she lives with her husband and Japanese koi in a blue house in Toronto. For more information visit rinasingh.com or follow her on Twitter and Instagram @storiesbysingh.

Ishita Jain is an illustrator from Delhi, India, though she is now based in New York. She is an alumnus of the National Institute of Design, Ahmedabad, India, and the MFA Illustration as Visual Essay Program at the School of Visual Arts, New York. Ishita loves to draw on location and enjoys documenting the people, places, and stories that surround her. Her work is inspired by day-to-day moments and the wonder that comes from being around nature. Her work can be seen at www.ishitajain.in and Instagram @ishitajain24.

Text copyright © 2023 by Rina Singh
Illustrations copyright © 2023 by Ishita Jain

First published in the United States, Great Britain, Canada, Australia, and New Zealand in 2023 by NorthSouth Books, Inc., an imprint of NordSüd Verlag AG, CH-8050 Zürich, Switzerland.

Distributed in the United States by NorthSouth Books, Inc., New York 10016.
Library of Congress Cataloging-in-Publication Data is available.
ISBN: 978-0-7358-4505-3
Printed in China
1 3 5 7 9 • 10 8 6 4 2
www.northsouth.com

The Forest Keeper

The true story of Jadav Payeng

by Rina Singh
illustrated by Ishita Jain

North South

1979. The river had behaved badly.
It burst over its banks and scattered hundreds of water snakes on the sandbar. In the burning, hot sun, without any tree cover, they shriveled up and died. Jadav, a tribal boy, raced to the edge of his river island and stood speechless.

Saddened, he ran to the elders for help and begged them to grow trees so the roots could hold on to the land.
"Trees don't grow on sandbars," they said with the sorrow of a thousand monsoons. He rushed to the forest department, but people who worked there were not interested. They gave him a bag with some bamboo seedlings.
"Go plant them yourself!"

Jadav hugged the bag and traveled to the river's many little islands and chose an abandoned one to grow the seedlings. He was sixteen years old when he planted his first bamboo.

Every day he took the bamboo seedlings, a stick,
and a bucket and rode his bike to the river.

Thud! Thud! Thud!
All day long he dug holes in the sandy soil and planted the
seedlings. His hands bruised and his shoulders ached, but he dug,
and he planted. He made hundreds of trips to the river to bring
water to tend the growing seedlings. It wasn't easy. In fact, it was
an impossible task. But he was not one to give up.

Then he took a boat to cross the river to reach the island.

Jadav thought of another way to water them. He built a bamboo platform above each sapling. He placed on it an earthen pot pierced with tiny holes and filled it with water.
The drip from the holes watered the saplings slowly.
This gave him time to plant more.

Day after day. Month after month. Year after year.
In time the bamboo shoots grew tall and turned into a huge thicket.

Jadav began to plant trees of many species.

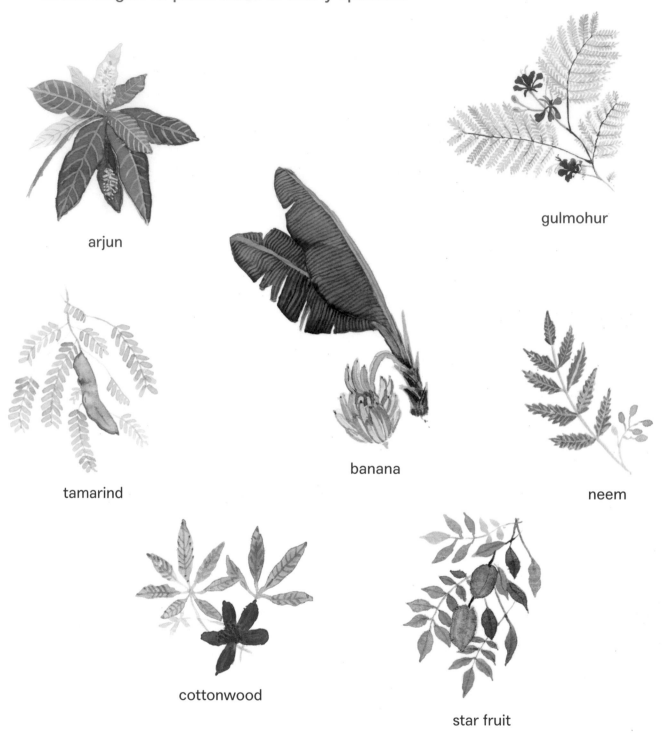

arjun

gulmohur

tamarind

banana

neem

cottonwood

star fruit

Monsoons came and went.
The wind and the river helped disperse seeds to other parts of the island.
And a forest was born.

The forest came alive the day
the birds came.
Pelicans and thrushes.
Woodpeckers and peacocks.
Eagles and vultures.

Then the animals crossed the river and wandered in,
looking for a home.

Wild boar and deer.
Rabbits and foxes.
Rhinos and tigers.

And one day some elephants
ambled into the forest.
Jadav stood back for the first time
and watched in awe the wonder
he had created.

But one night some hungry elephants,
desperate for food, strayed from his forest into
a neighboring village and smashed into huts.
The villagers ran and screamed.

The next day the villagers came armed with axes, threatening to cut down the forest.

"Cut me first before you touch
my forest!" he dared them.
"If we see another elephant in
our village again, we will
burn your forest to the ground!"
They warned him and left.
Jadav sighed with relief.

When the elephants migrated, he wondered and worried if they would return to his forest again.

To his pride and joy, they did.
Every year.

He made sure his forest was filled
with fruit trees and enough grass
so the elephants wouldn't wander
off into villages, looking for food.
Looking for trouble.

Thirty years passed.
Jadav and the world forgot about
each other. The river watched
the tribal boy become a forest man.
Whenever he stood in his forest
and looked, he saw creatures creeping,
crawling, jumping, and flying.
He listened to the humming of insects,
the songs of birds, and the distant
roar of tigers.
From the floor to the tops of the tallest
trees, Jadav's forest buzzed with life.
It still does.

The river floods from time to time, but Jadav's
trees stand tall and guard the island.

India

In a remote corner of northeast India, in Assam, there is
an island called Majuli. It's considered the world's largest river
island even though the Brahmaputra River has gouged out
half its landmass. There are many smaller islands around Majuli
that are also threatened by the river.

Jadav Molai Payeng, a tribesman from Majuli, has since 1979
planted a forest on an abandoned sandbar where nothing
had grown before. It was a wasteland. He labored in isolation
and complete anonymity, and his forest grew so gradually that
it went unnoticed for thirty years. His forest stretches over
1,359 acres of land, which is larger than Central Park in
New York.

The forest has become a migration corridor for a herd of more
than a hundred elephants.

In 2009, a wildlife photographer accidentally stumbled into
his forest, and since then Jadav has been written about, filmed,
and honored with many awards. He is known as the Forest Man
of India.

When Jadav turned thirty-nine, the tribal elders insisted he get
married and he did. He now lives with his wife and three children
who support his dream of planting more trees. He continues
to be the keeper of his forest, which is now named after him:
the Molai Forest.